Looking at Animal Parts

Let's Look at Animal Teeth

by Wendy Perkins

Consulting Editor: Gail Saunders-Smith, PhD

Consultant: Suzanne B. McLaren, Collections Manager
Section of Mammals, Carnegie Museum of Natural History
Edward O'Neil Research Center, Pittsburgh, Pennsylvania

Capstone
press®

Mankato, Minnesota

Pebble Plus is published by Capstone Press,
151 Good Counsel Drive, P.O. Box 669, Mankato, Minnesota 56002.
www.capstonepress.com

1 2 3 4 5 6 11 10 09 08 07 06

Library of Congress Cataloging-in-Publication Data
Perkins, Wendy, 1957–
    Let's look at animal teeth / by Wendy Perkins.
    p. cm.—(Pebble plus. Looking at animal parts)
    Summary: "Simple text and photographs present animal teeth, how they work, and how different animals
use them"—Provided by publisher.
    Includes bibliographical references and index.
    ISBN-13: 978-0-7368-6353-7 (hardcover)
    ISBN-10: 0-7368-6353-2 (hardcover)
    1. Teeth—Juvenile literature. I. Title. II. Series.
QL858.P38 2007
591.4'4—dc22
                                                           2006001001

Editorial Credits
Sarah L. Schuette, editor; Kia Adams, set designer; Renée Doyle, cover production; Kelly Garvin, photo
    researcher/photo editor

Photo Credits
Corbis/Kevin Schaefer, 14–15
Getty Images Inc./The Image Bank/Gallo Images-Heinrich van den Berg, cover
James P. Rowan, 20–21
Lynn M. Stone, 6–7, 8–9, 17
McDonald Wildlife Photography/Joe McDonald, 4–5
Seapics/James D. Watt, 18–19
Shutterstock/RHSR, 1
Tom & Pat Leeson, 10–11, 13

Note to Parents and Teachers

The Looking at Animal Parts set supports national science standards related to
life science. This book describes and illustrates animal teeth. The images support
early readers in understanding the text. The repetition of words and phrases helps early
readers learn new words. This book also introduces early readers to subject-specific
vocabulary words, which are defined in the Glossary section. Early readers may need
assistance to read some words and to use the Table of Contents, Glossary, Read More,
Internet Sites, and Index sections of the book.

Table of Contents

Teeth at Work

Animals bite, tear, and chew
with their teeth.
Animals use their teeth
to fight and scare
other animals away.

Chomp! A wolf kills its prey
with one bite.
Meat-eaters have sharp teeth.

A cow clips
a mouthful of grass.

She chews and chews.

Plant-eaters have flat teeth.

Kinds of Teeth

Beavers have
two long front teeth.
Beavers gnaw on trees
and cut them down.

Giraffes have many
wide, flat teeth.
They grind tough leaves
from tree tops.

Walruses have two tusks
outside their mouths.
Walruses fight
with their tusks.

Snakes have hollow fangs.

Snakes bite their food,

but they don't chew.

They swallow food whole.

Sharks have many rows
of very sharp teeth.
If one tooth falls out,
a new one grows
in its place.

Awesome Animal Teeth

Long or short,
sharp or flat,
teeth help animals
stay alive.

Glossary

fang—a long, pointed tooth

gnaw—to keep biting on something

grind—to crush into smaller pieces; some animals that eat plants have to grind their food to make it easier to swallow.

hollow—having an empty space inside; venom flows out of hollow snake teeth.

prey—an animal that is hunted for food

tusk—a long, curved, pointed tooth outside of the mouth; walruses and elephants have two tusks.

Read More

LaBella, Susan. *Beavers and Other Animals with Amazing Teeth.* Scholastic News Nonfiction Readers. New York: Children's Press, 2005.

Lynch, Wayne. *Whose Teeth Are These?* Name That Animal! Milwaukee: Gareth Stevens, 2003.

Miles, Elizabeth. *Mouths and Teeth.* Animal Parts. Chicago: Heinemann Libary, 2003.

Internet Sites

FactHound offers a safe, fun way to find Internet sites related to this book. All of the sites on FactHound have been researched by our staff.

Here's how:

1. Visit *www.facthound.com*

2. Choose your grade level.

3. Type in this book ID **0736863532** for age-appropriate sites. You may also browse subjects by clicking on letters, or by clicking on pictures and words.

4. Click on the **Fetch It** button.

FactHound will fetch the best sites for you!

Index

Word Count: 133
Grade: 1
Early-Intervention Level: 14